The Magic Castle Still Stands

Performing Rights

Applications for performance, including reading and excerpts, by amateurs and professionals in English should be addressed in first instance to the Playwright, Vanessa Frances, performancesvfrances@gmail.com

No performance of any kind may be given unless a license has been obtained. Applications should be made before rehearsals begin, Publication of this play does not necessarily indicate it's availability for performance.

*This play is dedicated to my thirteen-year-old
and twenty-two-year-old selves.*

The Magic Castle Still Stands

Vanessa Frances

PRODUCTION HISTORY

The Magic Castle Still Stands made its world premiere at Orlando Fringe 2024 at the Orlando Family Stage, in Orlando Florida, on May 18th, 2024. It was directed by Emily Kucala. The scenic and technical design was led by Andy Renae. It was also stage-managed by Andy Renae. The cast was:

Harvey	Amelia Reed Bryant
Iris	Victoria Lobdell
Donna	Yinelly Pastrana
Lewis	Carlos Cortes
Jack	Matthew Villegas
May	Courtney Cunningham
Mikey	Ella Hadley
Sammi	Kira Humphrey

CAST OF CHARACTERS

HARVEY: Twenty-something artist, female, quiet. Any ethnicity.

IRIS: Twenty-something, spacey, eternal optimist. Any ethnicity.

DONNA: Late 50s, woman, rampant attitude. Any ethnicity.

LEWIS: Sage-type, 70-something elderly man. Any ethnicity.

JACK: Train conductor, stoic, mid-30s. Any ethnicity.

MAY: Mother, late twenties, orderly. Any ethnicity.

MIKEY: May's daughter, young girl, any ethnicity.

SAMMI: Young girl, spacey, eternal optimist, any ethnicity.

SETTING

A train car departing from Savannah, GA. Dead of summer.

Act 1

Scene 1

Setting: *Mid-afternoon from the inside of a train car*

At Rise: *Harvey, climbs on board, carrying
a backpack. Harvey pulls a copy of Perks
of Being a Wallflower from her backpack,
looking over the front cover.*

*Lewis, sits down beside Harvey. May eyes
them both but turns back to her laptop,
handing Mikey, an iPad.*

MIKEY

I want to play with Sammi.

MAY

(tight lipped) Sammi thinks you should settle in... We're
gonna be on the train a while.

MIKEY

(unconvinced) Sammi didn't say that.

Turning to nudge her imaginary friend.

MIKEY

You wanna play, right?

MAY

Sit Mikey.

MIKEY
(to an imaginary Sammi, laughing)
No, Dr. Thomas says we can't call mom May, that's against
the rules. That's what *dad* calls her. And those other names.

MAY
(curt) Mikey, don't make me ask you again.

*Mikey begrudingly sits down. Train conductor Jack climbs
through the door with Donna hobbling behind. Donna
throws her bag into the overhead area and plops down in an
unoccupied row. Jack starts scanning tickets.*

JACK
(to Donna) Destination?

DONNA
You *know* where I'm going.

JACK
I still have to verify your ticket.

DONNA
You *saw* it.

JACK
I have to verify it now that we're onboard.

*Donna holds her ticket out to Jack, who scans it and returns
it to her.*

JACK
Thank you Mrs. Westbrook.

DONNA

(cold) Donna is *fine*. Westbrook is my ex-husband's name.

JACK

(eye rolling) Noted.

Donna huffs and sinks back into her seat. Jack approached May and scans her and Mikey's ticket, and finally Harvey and Lewis.

Harvey, has been listening to the other conversations and hastily holds out her ticket. Jack scans Harvey's ticket, writing a note and placing it in the place above the row.

JACK

(looking at Harvey's ticket) New York?

LEWIS

I'm headed that way too.

HARVEY

Oh, nice.

LEWIS

You been to the city before?

HARVEY

I haven't.

LEWIS

New York is unlike anywhere in the world. Everything you could imagine, just within reach.

HARVEY

(laughs) A friend of mine used to say that a lot.

JACK

(handing Lewis his ticket) Thanks.

LEWIS

Lewis. Nice to meet you—

HARVEY

Harvey.

Jack exits to the next cabin. They train starts to move forward.

DONNA

Excuse me—

LEWIS

Yes?

DONNA

Do we get a meal on this train?

LEWIS

Not in Coach. But there's a snack car in the back.

DONNA

Great.

Donna stands up and grabs her bag, but winces as she strains her leg.

DONNA

(huffs) My daughter said taking the train was *easier* than flying, but I'm starting to think she was full of *shit*.

LEWIS

Are you alright?

DONNA

Obviously not. *(beat)* I— *(sitting down)* tripped and broke
my leg in the garden last month... I can't drive or fly so, I'm
stuck *here.*

LEWIS

It's not bad once we get moving. Beautiful scenery. We're
going to pass an outstanding nature preserve. Shame it's the
summer. In the spring it's full of flowers.

DONNA

(intrigued) Flowers?

LEWIS

Hundreds. If there was a stop close to it, I'd go in and get
some for my daughter, straight from the source.

DONNA

(colder) Everybody says they like flowers. They just don't
like them enough to *pay* for them.

LEWIS

I still buy flowers.

DONNA

You're a rarity. *(beat)* Everybody wants shit to be
permanent. Flowers, are not.

MAY

Excuse me—

DONNA

Yes?

MAY

Would you keep the swearing to a minimum, around my daughter?

DONNA

I wasn't talking to you.

MAY

But we can *hear* you.

DONNA

Fine. Sorry. Small compartment.

MAY

Thanks.

Donna continues, lowering her voice.

LEWIS

I'd take the train over flying any day, (*beat*) See how beautiful it is? You can't get a good view of the sky from inside it.

Donna huffs and digs through her purse, biting into a granola bar.

DONNA

(*mouth full*) Besides, if I'm going to sleep, why does it matter what I can see outside?

LEWIS

(*shrugs*) Depends on what you want to wake up to.

Mikey giggles out towards the window, interacting with an imaginary friend. May shushes her.

MIKEY

I'm just talking to Sammi—

MAY

Mikey, Sammi— *(beat)* Just settle down, please?

Mikey restlessly looks around the train, and spies the cover of Harvey's book, pointing.

MIKEY

(to Harvey) That's a weird picture.

MAY

Mikey— *(to Harvey)* Sorry.

Harvey looks down at the cover.

HARVEY

It is a *little* weird.

MIKEY

(staring) Green is my favorite color.

HARVEY

Mine too.

MIKEY

But that's a *lot* of green. Like, too much.

HARVEY

It is a *lot* of green.

MIKEY

My dad says, sometimes you can have too much of a good thing, like candy or soda. Then you get sick.

HARVEY

Your dad's right.

MIKEY

(to the window) What do you think Sammi?

Mikey giggles

MIKEY

Hey! Sammi, cut it out!

MAY

(embarassed) Come on, leave her be.

HARVEY

Don't worry about it.

MAY

Kid stuff, you know?

Mikey pops up in her seat, looking as if she's playing with another kid.

MIKEY

Sammi! *(laughing)*

MAY

Mikey! Sit down. *Now.*

MIKEY

But-

May gives Mikey a stern look. Her face falls and she sinks into herchair. Donna, unfazed with Mikey, looks back at Lewis and Harvey.

LEWIS

My daughter lives in Poughkeepsie. I'm meeting her girlfriend for the first time. *(unfazed)* She's a florist.

DONNA

(frowning) Like I said, there's no money in flowers.

LEWIS

We're going to one of the best restaurants in Poughkeepsie and then into the city for the day. *(bright)* They have crab cakes.

DONNA

Hm. *(chewing her granola bar)* I'm so hungry, I'd take a Poughkeepsie crab cake. *(to Harvey)* What about you?

Donna speaks louder. Harvey is in her head.

DONNA

Hey!

Harvey turns.

HARVEY

Oh— *(looking between Lewis and Donna)* Visiting family.

DONNA

Didn't want to fly?

HARVEY

Flying makes me uncomfortable.

DONNA

You'll get used to it when you're older.

Donna takes out her phone. Lewis leans back and closes his eyes. The landscape rolls by outside the train window when suddenly the horn blasts at full volume and we hear a crash. The train lurches to a halt.

DONNA

What the fuck—

MAY

Please—!

MIKEY

(bright) Fuck!

May puts her hand over Mikey's mouth.

MAY

Don't say that.

MIKEY

Sammi says I can say it.

MAY

(her jaw tenses) I don't think *Sammi* should be speaking for you and *especially* not for me.

Mikey leans over, almost like she is speaking to somebody else, frowning.

DONNA

(to her phone) Siri, call Casey, I want off this train.

SIRI

Sorry, did you say— "Google T-Pain?"

DONNA

Why would I—

Donna dials her phone. Commotion ensues. Jack rushes in.

LEWIS

What's going on?

JACK

We're stopping temporarily.

DONNA

Are you kidding me? *(sharp)* I've had enough.

Donna stands up.

JACK

Ma'am—

DONNA

(into her phone) I want out of here. Casey, I can't *believe* you put me on this God-foresaken train. Call your brother and tell him—

Jack hesitantly reaches out to stop Donna.

JACK

Legally, I can't let you off this train if we're not stopped at a station.

Donna's face hardens. She looks to her phone, closing the call.

DONNA

I'll talk to you later.

JACK

(to everyone) There's been an incident on the tracks.

LEWIS

Is everyone okay?

MAY

(looking out) Is that... A car?

Everyone rushes over to look.

HARVEY

Oh my God.

May pulls Mikey away from the window.

DONNA

(to Jack) Did you not see them? Barreling towards us? *(looking out the window)* Looks like a lawsuit if I've ever seen one.

Jack ignores her and starts walking through the cabin.

JACK

Please return to your seats.

Jack exits.

MIKEY

What happened?

MAY

We're stuck here for a little bit. *(handing her back her iPad)* Shouldn't be long.

MIKEY

Can I play cars?

MAY

Not right now.

MIKEY

But Sammi—

MAY

(mad) Mikey.

MIKEY

Sorry.

Mikey slumps down. Donna huffs.

MAY

(firm) Do you have something to say?

DONNA

Nope.

MAY

Good. *(beat)* I'm sure this was just an accident.

DONNA

Accident or not, we're gonna be here a while. Might as well keep your kid entertained with... Whatever she's going on about.

MAY

I need to get her to her dad's house. *(beat)* Does this kind of thing usually last very long?

DONNA

It's Amtrak.

LEWIS

(gentle) Hopefully not.

MAY

(beat) I'll get in trouble if I keep Mikey for too long.

LEWIS

I'm sure there's a way to contact them and explain the situation.

MAY

Maybe I can— *(typing into her computer)* Wifi's out. *(exhausted)* Shit.

DONNA

(coy) Excuse me, watch your mouth, please—

MAY

Oh shut up! You've done nothing but complain this whole time. Some of us have serious stuff going on.

DONNA

And me breaking my leg and being unable to fly *isn't* serious?

MAY

Stop talking to me. *Seriously.*

May takes out her phone and starts texting.

LEWIS

(taking a deep breath) Just terrible.

DONNA

Either we've got a case of an idiot driving straight through the crossing without looking for a train, or— *(frowning)* a crazy person trying to throw themselves in front of it.

LEWIS

This kind of thing is usually an accident—

HARVEY

Do you have to talk like that?

DONNA

Like what?

HARVEY

Seems kind of insensitive.

DONNA

Just calling it like I see it.

HARVEY

We don't know the situation.

DONNA

Do you?

HARVEY

I don't have to know the situation to know you shouldn't talk like that.

Donna leans back in her seat. Harvey flips through the pages of her book.

DONNA

(beat) My bet's on suicide.

HARVEY

Okay, can you shut up?

DONNA

I don't see why you're getting defensive over a stranger.

HARVEY

I don't care if they're a stranger. Suicide is... Awful.

DONNA

See, when I was your age, these people were put into institutions, and away from the rest of us.

HARVEY

I didn't know I was talking to the all-knowing.

DONNA

Maybe I don't know, but, I do know there are ways to cope that aren't throwing your life away selfishly and inconveniencing everyone around you.

HARVEY

Selfishly?—

LEWIS

(calm, interrupting) I think we all just need to take a deep breath. At least the scenery is nice.

Pause

DONNA

What a lovely gas station.

LEWIS

There's a meadow too.

Enter Jack.

MAY

Any updates?

JACK

We're holding here until we get clearance.

DONNA

Something to investigate?

JACK

(beat) I can't confirm anything right now.

DONNA

(smug) Called it.

HARVEY

(standing) You know what-

LEWIS

Hey—

MAY

Oh—

DONNA

My son told me there were crazy people on the train.

HARVEY

(intensifying, almost to a frightening extent) You have SO much nerve to talk about people that way when you don't even know them. Do you know how unfeeling you sound?

DONNA

(indifferent) Like I said, they should've kept the institutions open.

Harvey starts to object.

JACK

Excuse me! I'll remove you both from the train at the next station if you can't settle down.

DONNA

(relief) Thank God.

HARVEY

(panic) Wait, no I—

DONNA

(condescending) Just have your family from New York come get you.

JACK

And you need to watch your language and your behavior.

The overhead intercom buzzes.

OVERHEAD VOICE

Attention passengers, we're holding temporarily. Thanks for your patience.

Jack pulls his radio off his belt.

JACK

(into the radio) I'll be right up. *(to Donna and Harvey)* Are we clear about the expectations here?

DONNA

Crystal.

Harvey nods. Jack exits.

LEWIS

(to Harvey) You alright?

HARVEY

Yeah— I just—I have to get out of here.

LEWIS

Georgia?

HARVEY

(beat) It's hard to explain.

LEWIS

(nodding) Let me know if you change your mind.

Lewis nods and tilts his head back to sleep. Harvey looks at her book before going to sleep. She tosses and turns. The light in the cabin flashes red before returning to normal. Laughter from offstage. Harvey awakens and walks through the cabin and off stage.

Fade to black

Scene 2

Setting: *Empty train car, the lights are red*

At Rise: *Lights up into the empty train car. Harvey walks in, looking around.*

       Iris enters from stage left, reading from Harvey's book. Harvey doesn't see Iris until she turns back around. They mirror each other's stances.

IRIS

(reading) "And even if somebody else has it much worse, that doesn't really change the fact that you have what you have. Good and bad." *(beat)* That's depressing.

HARVEY

(beat) (shocked) Iris?

IRIS grins.

IRIS

Hi Harvey.

HARVEY

(disbelief) I thought—

Iris looks back down at the book.

IRIS

I don't think I ever finished this book.*(laughs)* Do you think I'd like the ending?

HARVEY

I— How did I—What are you doing here?

IRIS

(looking up from the book) We'll have time to catch up.
(beat) Tell me about this book! Don't be afraid to spoil it!

HARVEY

This isn't funny.

Harvey and Iris mirror each other's mannerisms without noticing. They step at the same time, Harvey much more frantic than Iris.

IRIS

(looking back at the book) The biggest critique I have of this book is— *(laughs)*, Listen to me! I sound like... Your mom or something. *(beat)* I don't remember half the things she used to talk—

Harvey flinches at the mention of her mom.

IRIS

(realizing) Sorry, I didn't—

HARVEY

(firm) What are you doing here?

IRIS

(ignores, tone is light again) You always had to explain stuff like this to me—

HARVEY

Stop it, you bought this when we were in high school—

IRIS

I—

HARVEY

What are you doing here? How did you even get here?

IRIS

Jeez, relax. I've just been waiting for you to show up! *(beat)* You've had a tough twenty-four hours.

HARVEY

How would you know that?

IRIS

I had a gut feeling.

Iris places her hand on Harvey's forehead.

HARVEY

(shoving Iris) Why are you here?

IRIS

Good question, you first.

HARVEY

(beat) That's not how this works.

IRIS

You don't remember the question game?

HARVEY

We're not playing a game.

IRIS

(disappointed) Hmph. Well... Everyone's worried sick you left without telling anyone.

HARVEY

(beat) You don't know that.

IRIS

Gut feeling, remember?

HARVEY

I don't wanna talk about this, especially not with you.

IRIS

Harv, come on! Wanna... Play Kingdom or something?

HARVEY

Don't— *(beat)* You gotta leave.

IRIS

Where should I go?

Harvey starts walking towards the door.

HARVEY

Fine, I'll leave.

Iris grabs Harvey's wrist as she starts to leave.

IRIS

Come on, let's do something fun. *(beat)* It's been so boring without you. I don't have anyone to talk to.

HARVEY

Tough.

IRIS

It's been... A month now? Two? Since I've seen you?

HARVEY

(cold) Three.

IRIS

(soft) That long?

HARVEY

Assumed you'd noticed.

IRIS

Don't be like that.

HARVEY

Don't be like that? *(pulling her wrist away)*

Harvey walks towards the door between cabins but she realizes it's locked. The lights inside the train flicker and blink from bright to red, trapped between realities.

HARVEY

What's happening? *(beat)* What did you do?

IRIS

(aback) How is this is my fault?

HARVEY

It usually is.

IRIS

That's not true. *(beat)* A lot of stuff is also your fault.

HARVEY

(looking around) Thanks for the reminder.

IRIS

(indifferent) In case you didn't notice, you're being a real bitch. I came all this way to see you.

Harvey ignores her and bangs on the door. The lights flicker.

HARVEY

Hello? What's going on? Is there anyone out there? *(beat)* Jack? Lewis? May? *(beat)* Donna?

IRIS

(looking up) Did you make some friends? Will I get to meet them?

HARVEY

They're not my friends.

IRIS

First name basis sounds like friends.

HARVEY

They're just people on the train.

IRIS

And I was just someone you played with in elementary school. *(grinning, getting closer to Harvey)* And look where we are now!

HARVEY

Stop talking.

IRIS

Best friends—

HARVEY

Knock it off—

IRIS

—Forever!

HARVEY

You are not my friend Iris!

IRIS

(beat) What?

HARVEY

You're not.

IRIS

(ignores) Are you sure you wouldn't feel better if we played Kingdom? It used to cheer you up. *(beat)* You remember, right?

Harvey walks around the cabin, pressing on windows, trying to find a way out.

IRIS

We'd go to the old Orchid World building with the open roof... You could count all the stars at night. Remember when we got an orchid to bloom once? *(laughs)* Felt like Christmas.

Harvey's jaw tightens, but she ignores Iris. She bangs on the door.

HARVEY

Hello? Can anyone hear me?

Harvey frantically walks through the cabin, trying every window. Iris is indifferent.

IRIS
Laying under the sky, imagining the New York apartment we'd get when we were out of school. *(beat)* Our own castle. Quiet. Bookshelves from floor to ceiling, with green walls! You were going to be an artist full-time... *(beat)* Remember?

Harvey freezes at one of the windows. Iris looks over patiently.

IRIS
I remember.

Harvey turns around and charges at Iris, pushing her down in the seat, shaking her shoulders.

HARVEY
Shut. Up. Stop fucking talking.

IRIS
Come on Harv—

HARVEY
Grow up! We're not kids anymore.

IRIS
Then what am I doing here?

HARVEY
That's what I asked you—

IRIS

I mean, you're here... Aren't you? Why wouldn't I be?

Harvey freezes. Iris pulls Harvey in to kiss her. Harvey softens but then slaps Iris across the face. Iris grins and reaches for Harvey's hand as it slips from her cheek.

IRIS

(beat) Your palms so calloused now.

Harvey pulls her hand back and steps away from Iris.

HARVEY

(mad) You disappeared. *(beat)* And no one could tell me what happened to you—*(beat)* Am I supposed to just forget that?

IRIS

We were changing. So... Fast.

HARVEY

That's not the whole truth and you know it.

IRIS

What do you—

HARVEY

You know exactly what I'm talking about Iris. You know exactly when everything went to shit. The truth is, when the fun and games were over, when the daydream was over, you were done. *(beat)* With me.

IRIS

(soft) You disappeared from me too.

HARVEY

I waited for you for hours, begging for you to show up and you didn't. *(beat)* You can't sit here and ask me to... Play Kingdom like it wasn't you that made everything fall apart.

Harvey begins to get visibly emotional.

HARVEY

(sad but disgusted) I didn't know if you were dead. I— *(beat)* It doesn't matter, I don't owe you the explanation, of all people.

IRIS

(quiet) Does it help that I'm not dead?

HARVEY

You've been dead to me.

IRIS

(beat) Please— I want— I want things to be okay. I want to be with you again.

Iris reaches for Harvey's arm again, running her hand up her shoulder. Harvey tries to hold firm, but her eyes slide across Iris' arm.

HARVEY

I—

The train rattles, the red light flickering and then shutting off. Harvey pulls her arm away from Iris, and drops it to her side. Harvey pulls on the cabin door again. It is unlocked.

HARVEY

I gotta go.

Iris runs towards Harvey.

IRIS

Harvey *(beat)* Please... Stay.

Harvey looks Iris over and then pushes open the door.

Cut to black.

Scene 3

Setting: *The main train cabin, mid-afternoon*

At Rise: *Lights come back up on the original cabin, Harvey steps inside, and stops in the middle of the aisle.*

MAY

(to Harvey) Any news?

Harvey struggles to hide her confusion.

LEWIS

Are you okay? You look like you've seen a ghost. *(beat)* Did you?

HARVEY

I—I don't know.

Harvey looks around the cabin and then down at her feet. Her book is gone.

HARVEY

Did someone sit here?

LEWIS

Not since you left.

Harvey dives down looking for her book.

LEWIS

What?

HARVEY

Did you see my book?

Harvey panics, scrambling out of her chair and scavenging around the floor of the cabin.

HARVEY

(anxious) Where's my book?

LEWIS

I'm sure it can't be far. It's not like it got up and walked off the train. *(to everyone)* Any of you see a book on the floor? Might have slid around...

Everyone besides Donna starts looking for the book

HARVEY

Did she—

LEWIS

She?

HARVEY

She has my book.

LEWIS

Who—

HARVEY

I—

Harvey stands up and starts walking back towards the cabin door.

HARVEY

I'll just go get it—

Enter Jack through the door.

JACK

Miss, we asked everyone to stay in their seats until we got this situation resolved.

HARVEY

I know—I'm sorry, I think my book's in the next cabin-

JACK

We need you to stay seated.

HARVEY

(frustrated) It'll only take a minute—

JACK

You can look once we give the all clear.

HARVEY

Please—

JACK

Miss, sit.

                                MAY

(to Jack) What happened out there?

Jack takes a deep breath.

                                JACK

(beat) It looks like she stopped on the tracks—

Harvey looks up.

                              HARVEY

She?

                               DONNA

I can tell you, I'm sure it wasn't an accident.

                                MAY

I don't know if I'd be happy to be right about that.

                               DONNA

A guess is a guess.

                                MAY

I don't wish this on anyone.

                               DONNA

What can we do about it? Keep sitting here?

                                MAY

No, but... Think about that girl's family. Would you want
your kid to go through that?

                               DONNA

I didn't raise mine to think that's an option.

May leans over and cover's Mikey's ears.

MIKEY

Hey!

MAY

(whispering) I don't think suicide is an option anyone teaches their kids.

DONNA

Sure, but some of us remind them to be strong. No wonder some people turn out the way they do. *(beat)* Can't grow up, can't let go.

May turns back around in her seat, lowering her hands off Mikey's ears.

MIKEY

(laughing) Come on Sammi—

MAY

Mikey... Please.

May puts her hand on top of Mikey's head.

HARVEY

(to Jack) What was her name?

JACK

We can't give out that information.

HARVEY

I think—

JACK

Please have a seat, we should get moving shortly.

*Harvey walks over and slumps back down in her seat,
turning her eyes out towards the window. Jack exits.*

MAY

I've only seen stuff like this on the news...

LEWIS

(beat) My daughter was hit by a train when she was a kid.

MAY

What?

LEWIS

She was playing outside with her friends. We heard the
sound of the horn in the distance but didn't think anything
of it. Thought she knew better, thought we *taught* her better..
But sometimes... Kids just get caught in their own world.
(beat) By some miracle, she survived, and now, I take the
train north to see her.

MAY

I'd never get on a train again.

LEWIS

I'm forming new associations with trains. Happy ones.
As hard as it was in the beginning, it's worth it. *(beat)* No
confinement to memory for me. It helps me stay in control
of my own life.

HARVEY

(beat) I don't know what I'm doing most of the time even if
I am in control.

LEWIS

(soft) Does anyone?

HARVEY

Most adults seem to.

LEWIS

Are you not an adult?

HARVEY

Doesn't feel like it.

LEWIS

What does it mean to be an adult to you?

HARVEY

(beat) I'm not sure.

LEWIS

Have you traveled alone before?

HARVEY

(beat) I've never left Georgia before.

LEWIS

Traveling is something adults do. Making their own choices
is too. Even if they don't know if they're the right ones.
(beat) Adulthood is just adaptation.

Harvey looks at her shoes.

HARVEY

I've always wanted to go to New York. I'm not sure I
actually know anything real about it.

LEWIS

(grinning) It's a good time to find out.

Donna turns into the conversation.

DONNA

There's more to it than that.

LEWIS

Well of course, but she's just starting out.

DONNA

And we all did... But a lesson learned sooner rather than later is adulthood means you are truly alone. You have to take care of yourself, without depending on anyone. The easy days, they're over, and they never come back.

LEWIS

That's not—

DONNA

Really? Has anyone here had it easy? Hasn't had to make endless sacrifices? The world is bitter. *(to Harvey)* You're just getting your first taste.

Donna bites into her protein bar. Harvey sits back in her chair.

The train horn blares. Everyone looks around as the train starts to move forward, the landscape sliding across the faces of the passengers and through the windows. The crashed car is fully in view. May cover's Mikey's eyes.

MIKEY

Why can't I see?

MAY

You just... Can't.

Harvey is in shock as she stands at the window.

HARVEY

(beat) There's no way that could have been—No. No no—

Harvey rushes away from the window.

LEWIS

Harvey—

HARVEY

(frantic) Stop the train! Please—

DONNA

Here we go—

HARVEY

(frantic) I— My book- Maybe it fell outside or something...
I just-

DONNA

How could your stuff be out there? *(sarcastic)* Were you
driving the car?

HARVEY

But—

DONNA

You're imagining it.

LEWIS

(gentle) You haven't been off the train, have you?

HARVEY

No, I don't— I don't think, but she— *(stumbling over her words)* I don't know— She—I— Was she here?

LEWIS

Who's she?

HARVEY

A girl, about my age, traveling alone? I think she had my book.

DONNA

The only person stumbling around causing a problem has been you.

MAY

You're not helping. *(gentle)* Harvey, you've got yourself worked up, I'm sure the book is around here—

Harvey starts digging between the seats.

HARVEY

(quiet) She could have—

The train picks up speed landscapes rolling over the faces of each of the passengers, venturing forward until the car slowly disappears.

LEWIS

It'll turn up. Everything does.

Harvey's eyes lock on the projected scenes moving across the windows

LEWIS
You should be excited. We're going to New York.

HARVEY
(beat) I know.

The landscape is moving faster, the light casting over all of their faces as it accelerates, Harvey looking out into the house. The train horn blares.

Cut to black.

Scene 4

Setting: *The main train cabin, night*

At Rise: *The lights come up in the car,*
                   Harvey is the only one awake.

Jack enters the cabin. Harvey looks up.

JACK
If you don't have a pillow, balling up a jacket works.

HARVEY
Thanks.

Jack nods.

JACK
I've found trains to be pretty therapeutic. It's why I became a conductor. Wanted a job where I was always in motion.

HARVEY
It is really comforting to—

JACK
—race past it all?

Harvey nods.

HARVEY

I feel like I'm running from my own brain most days. It's weird seeing the scenery go by just as fast.

JACK

Your mind is the one landscape you'll always reside in.

Harvey stares at the window.

HARVEY

I wish it was nicer.

JACK

Try tilting your head.

HARVEY

(Harvey turns her head) Maybe.

JACK

(beat) That book means a lot to you.

HARVEY

(beat) Yeah... There's a note in the front cover from someone. I— I don't know. *(beat)* I think she— *(Harvey struggles to verbalize the situation)* I don't know. It's complicated.

Jack nods.

JACK

Most things that go missing are usually right where you expect to find them.

HARVEY

Feel like I've looked everywhere.

JACK

(beat) Try again in the morning.

HARVEY

(nodding) Thanks.

Harvey starts to slump over but turns back to Jack.

HARVEY

Hey— um...

Jack turns.

HARVEY

I don't know if you can tell me this but... Did that girl... Die?

Jack takes a deep breath.

JACK

(beat) No.

Harvey nods.

JACK

Kind of a miracle if you ask me.

Jack exits. Harvey tries to close her eyes. Mikey begins to stir, looking around before leaning over to talk to Harvey.

MIKEY

(to Harvey) Are you awake? Miss?

Harvey stirs.

                    HARVEY
Hi.

                    MIKEY
Did you find your book?

Harvey shakes her head.

                    HARVEY
No, not yet.

                    MIKEY
What's it about?

                    HARVEY
(beat) It's about... Someone who doesn't feel like they fit in.

                    MIKEY
Are they an alien?

                    HARVEY
No, they're just... Different. Like how you and I might be
different.

                    MIKEY
(nods) My mom says God made us different so He wouldn't
mix us up.

                    HARVEY
She might be right.

Mikey begins rolling a toy car across the seats.

MIKEY

Do you believe in God?

HARVEY

That's kind of a hard question.

MIKEY

(shrugs) One time, I brought my friend to Sunday School and the teacher told me that she had to leave. Now I have to talk to some lady. *(beat)* She's mean. Then, the court said I have to see my dad. *(beat)* And God I guess.

HARVEY

Do you like your dad?

Mikey nods.

MIKEY

He's... Loud. I don't know if he likes my friend either.

HARVEY

Why not?

MIKEY

He says we're disruptive and that I need to act like a big kid. *(beat)* It's hard.

HARVEY

It is hard.

Harvey nods.

MIKEY

Did you throw your book off the train?

Harvey laughs.

HARVEY

Sometimes I think I should get rid of that book but, no.

MIKEY

Is it a bad book?

HARVEY

No, it just... Was given to me by someone I have some bad memories with.

MIKEY

Maybe you can take the bad pages out.

HARVEY

Maybe.

Mikey frowns, gets out of her seat, and quickly tiptoes over.

MIKEY

Wanna play a game?

HARVEY

What kind of game?

MIKEY

What games do you know?

Harvey laughs.

HARVEY

I haven't played a game in a long time.

Mikey frowns.

MIKEY

That's boring.

HARVEY

It can be.

MIKEY

What do grownups do if they don't play games?

HARVEY

I— I don't know actually. *(beat)* I guess we play games that... Don't have winners.

MIKEY

Why do you play them then?

HARVEY

It's just... What you're supposed to do.

Mikey frowns.

MIKEY

My dad sometimes plays games with me.

HARVEY

That's good.

MIKEY

I wish we could play more, but they don't love each other anymore.

HARVEY

Your parents?

Mikey nods.

HARVEY

Doesn't mean they don't love you.

MIKEY

I know. My mom yells about him a lot.

HARVEY

That's not your fault.

MIKEY

If I was better, bad stuff wouldn't happen.

HARVEY

That's not true.

MIKEY

They'd fight less if I did better in school. Or if I wasn't so loud. Mom says I'm really loud. My teacher says that kids like me always act like this.

HARVEY

Kids like you?

MIKEY

Kids with "bad houses." *(beat)* I think our house is nice. It has green walls. They tried to say my dad was bad after he left but, he's not bad. *(beat)* We're all bad sometimes.

HARVEY

(beat) You know, I had a "bad house" too. But I knew even when things were scary, I had someone that was very important to me.

MIKEY

A best friend? What did you do together?

HARVEY

(beat) We played games. One was called "Kingdom" You pretended to be a knight or king or princess... It was a lot of fun... But... We got older, and stopped playing.

Mikey hands Harvey one of her cars. She absentmindedly begins driving it across her leg.

HARVEY

My teachers said I was loud too, so I had to get all my energy out on the playground until I didn't feel—

MIKEY

Buzzy!

HARVEY

(nodding) Buzzy.

MIKEY

(beat) You're not loud.

HARVEY

I've been working on it.

MIKEY

Are you still friends?

HARVEY

(beat) Sometimes friends just, grow apart.

MIKEY

(firm) I'm not gonna grow apart from my friends.

HARVEY

I hope you don't.

MIKEY

I play games with my friend Sammi.

HARVEY

What's Sammi like?

Mikey grins.

MIKEY

Sammi is my best friend. We do everything together. *(beat)* But sometimes she goes away for a long time and I don't see her.

HARVEY

(confused) Where does she go?

Mikey shrugs.

MIKEY

I don't know... But she always comes back! And we play for hours! And have sleepovers and race down my street or read in my backyard *(laughing)*. *(beat)* I don't like when she goes away.

HARVEY

It's not fun when your friends go away.

MIKEY

(Mikey nods) She's the best!

HARVEY

What games do you and Sammi play?

MIKEY

I can show you—

*Mikey waves out to house and Sammi comes running up to
the stage from the audience. The lights in the train begin
to flicker and then change to the same shade of red Harvey
saw earlier. Harvey stands up.*

HARVEY

What—

*Mikey returns with Sammi, another young girl. Harvey is
confused.*

Sammi grins.

SAMMI

Mikey is my best friend.

MIKEY

We're alike in every way.

SAMMI

I'm you!

MIKEY

And you're me!

*The two of them start shoving each other back and forth,
laughing. May stirs in her seat but doesn't wake up. The
other passengers are still.*

SAMMI

Someday... We're gonna build a log cabin.

MIKEY

And it's gonna have a HUGE waterslide and lots of rooms
for race cars.

SAMMI

And one BIG bedroom.

MIKEY

So that we're never apart!

The two girls laugh. Harvey scans the situation.

MIKEY

Not many people get to see Sammi, so you're very lucky.

HARVEY

What do you mean?

MIKEY

Nobody can see her! Just me, and now, you! That means
you must be special.

HARVEY

Does your mom know Sammi is here?

MIKEY

Of course! But she can't see her. *(beat)* Our favorite game is
chase!

*Sammi grins and tags Mikey, running down the train
corridor and laughing.*

MIKEY

See! She's the best. That's why she's coming with me!

Harvey is putting pieces together.

HARVEY

Mikey—

Harvey takes Mikey's hand. Sammi keeps running.

HARVEY

When did you meet Sammi?

Mikey frowns, looking down at her feet.

MIKEY

I don't remember.

Sammi looks annoyed that Mikey has been stopped and goes to Mikey's seat and starts going through her toy cars.

HARVEY

(soft) Are you sure?

Mikey digs her toes into the train floor.

MIKEY

Mom was crying and... They were yelling— *(beat, Mikey is having a hard time recalling the day)* I ran outside with my cars... *(beat)* Sammi was in the backyard and— now we're friends.

HARVEY

(beat) Does Sammi make you feel safe?

MIKEY

(breaks into a smile) Nothing bad happens with Sammi.

Sammi jumps up from the seat and runs back to Mikey.

SAMMI

And now we always play chase! And cars!

MIKEY

(grinning) And cars!

Harvey nods, tapping her fingers on the back of the chair.

HARVEY

It's really late... I think you two need to get some sleep.

Mikey and Sammi groan.

MIKEY

We're not tired!

SAMMI

I want to keep playing... Don't you Mikey?

Mikey nods.

MIKEY

We had to be quiet all day!

SAMMI

Not a peep!

MIKEY

I haven't even shown you my new cars yet.

SAMMI

New cars?!

MIKEY

There's a blue one and a green one—

HARVEY

Come on, don't wake your mom.

Mikey and Sammi sigh.

MIKEY

Okay... Goodnight.

SAMMI

It was nice to meet you!

HARVEY

(beat) You too.

Sammi rushes off to the chair but Mikey turns back to Harvey and hands her a car toy.

MIKEY

You can keep that car in case you don't find your book. So you have something to play with.

HARVEY

Thanks Mikey.

Mikey and Sammi return to the aisle seat. May begins to stir. The lights flicker between red and change back to normal. May sits up as Harvey walks towards the train cabin door.

MAY

(half-asleep) Did we stop again? I thought I heard something.

HARVEY

(shaking her head) No, it was probably me. Sorry about that. Can't sleep.

MAY

(nodding) This isn't exactly comfy.

Harvey starts to step towards the doors again but stops.

HARVEY

Do you... Know about Mikey's friend Sammi?

MAY

(sitting up) Sammi...? Oh— Sammi. Mikey's... 'Friend.'
Why do you ask?

HARVEY

She got up a little bit ago and was introducing me to her.

MAY

Mikey spends a lot of time in her head. *(beat)* Our family
counselor says it's a trauma response. Happens a lot to kids
that have... Been through something difficult.

May gently strokes Mikey's hair.

MAY

The divorce was hard on her. *(beat)* Mikey's really
dependent on Sammi. *(beat)* Sometimes I wish she would
just grow out of it, other times, I don't know what she'd
do without her. I suppose— At least, I hope, she'll be okay
when she's older.

HARVEY

(beat) (realization) I think she will.

Mikey rolls over.

MIKEY

Mom, did we pack Sammi's cars? I wanna race at dad's tomorrow with her.

Mikey gestures to a sleeping Sammi, and though May follows where Mikey is pointing, she makes it clear that she doesn't actually see her and is just playing along.

MAY

(putting her hand on Mikey's back) Of course.

May turns and winks at Harvey.

MAY

Alright sweetie, let's get back to sleep. You don't wanna be tired when you see your dad, do you?

MIKEY

(shaking her head) I guess.

MAY

(holding Mikey in her arms) Come on, you're going to have so much fun. Okay?

MAY

(turning to Harvey) Goodnight.

HARVEY

(knowing) Goodnight.

Harvey opens the door to the next cabin.

Cut to black.

Scene 5

Setting: *Empty train car, the lights are red*

At Rise: *Harvey reenters the cabin, the room is a
                  familiar shade of red.*

*Iris has her feet kicked up on a chair, but stands up when
she sees Harvey.*

IRIS
You're back.

HARVEY
I am.

IRIS
There's... So much that I want to explain to you. *(beat)* I
was just hoping I didn't have to.

HARVEY
I'll make it fun.

IRIS
Like... The question game?

HARVEY
Why not.

IRIS
You go first.

HARVEY
Okay. You showed up at my house when we were seven.

IRIS
Yup.

HARVEY
You told me you liked books and gardens and painting, just
like me.

IRIS

Because I do.

HARVEY

Right. You were at my house every afternoon. You moved in with me. *(beat)* And then we found the Orchid World building.

IRIS

(laughing) This doesn't sound like a question—

HARVEY

(ignoring) And we started playing Kingdom.

IRIS

(beat) I thought you didn't remember?

HARVEY

Of course I remember Kingdom. I was just... Afraid.

IRIS

Why?

HARVEY

Kingdom was more than a game to me. It was all I had... Most days. *(beat)* I could close my eyes and picture a place where things were... Steady. Where they made sense.

IRIS

(beat) What are you getting at?

HARVEY

(ignoring) Everything was good in Kingdom. I had a horse, we planted a garden. I swore there were days that the building did look like the castle we talked about.

HARVEY

Or the apartment we wanted. Looking through that open
ceiling like it was a portal to another universe. We went
back to that building for years and kept playing Kingdom.
Talking about it like... Like it was already real.

IRIS

We were also imagining a future! That's not Kingdom... It
was something that could happen. *(beat)* For us.

HARVEY

Then, you disappeared when we were supposed to make it
real.

IRIS

(beat) What if it wasn't everything we'd imagined?

HARVEY

Was it worth not trying?

IRIS

(beat) What's the question?

HARVEY

We had nothing real, Iris. We had an abandoned building,
with mold and dead flowers. *(beat)* They were building
a parking garage across the street, the light had already
flooded out the stars. *(beat)* We had an illusion, A— a
fantasy. An escape. *(beat)* You can't live there.

IRIS

But it meant so much more than that.

HARVEY

What did you expect us to do? Stay put until some developer tore it down?

IRIS

This question isn't fun Harvey—

HARVEY

I wanted more. I wanted something real.

Iris looks up.

IRIS

Was it not real to you?

HARVEY

(deep breath) Iris, the only real thing we had was that shell of a building and our shared room in my childhood home after—

IRIS

Please don't say it again, please—

Iris quickly crosses the stage covering her ears.

HARVEY

—my mom committed suicide. *(beat)* All that was left was you, me, and the past. I couldn't live there anymore, not for the sake of our emaciated daydream.

IRIS

I don't want to talk about this again. I don't want to—

Harvey rushes over and peels Iris' hands off her ears.

HARVEY

And that's it. That was the one part of me you could never accept. *(beat)* That I hurt. And it was real.

IRIS

(heavy) What was I supposed to do, Harvey? What was I supposed to say?

HARVEY

You were supposed to be my friend!

IRIS

I didn't... I didn't know... How to help...

HARVEY

You weren't meant to know. And at first, I didn't understand why— *(beat)* the one person in the world that was supposed to just understand me... Didn't. *(beat)* So.. I... got on this train to New York so I didn't have to go home... All I wanted was to make these fantasies into something tangible. And get away from... Everything else.

HARVEY

I really thought you were in that car. *(beat)* That I'd lost you forever and you'd come back to me as some weird ghost, but I know that's not it.

IRIS

I'm... Sorry Harvey.

HARVEY

No, I'm sorry. *(beat)* That I... Didn't understand.

Iris tilts her head.

HARVEY

I didn't understand why... Why you weren't in the car or at my house or on this train or anywhere I could have thought to look for you...

Harvey steps back.

HARVEY

The green walls, the art, the bookshelves, the open sky, even getting that damn orchid to finally bloom. *(beat)* It's just pretend. *(beat)* And so are you. *(beat)* Because... Are you me?

The red lights flicker and then fade to fill with the sunrise out of the windows from the rolling scenery outside.

IRIS

Is that your question?

HARVEY

Yes.

IRIS

(beat) Yes.

HARVEY

You didn't give me that book.

IRIS

(beat) No.

HARVEY

It's not your handwriting in the cover.

IRIS

(beat) No.

HARVEY

It's mine.

Iris nods.

HARVEY

You're the part of me I preserved. *(beat)* And you disappeared because—

IRIS

You were whole. *(beat)* Even if it didn't feel like it. You grew up. You were all of your parts, good and bad. *(beat)* You didn't need an extension of yourself. You were just... Harvey.

HARVEY

You knew?

IRIS

(nodding) I'm you, aren't I?

HARVEY

And every time I tried to fight it—

IRIS

I had to come back.

HARVEY

And once I... I commit to it— I— lose you. *(beat)* Forever.

IRIS

(beat) You don't really lose me. I just... become part of you.
The softer bits. Flowers.. Or paint or... Castles. *(beat)* It'll
just be different. A feeling, or, a memory.

HARVEY

(beat) I don't know who I'll be.

IRIS

You'll still be you! Just... Less disjointed.

HARVEY

It's hard to be sure.

IRIS

I don't think you have to be sure, you just have to be willing
to jump.

*Harvey plays with Mikey's car in her hand. Iris walks over
and takes Harvey's hands in her own.*

IRIS

Look at your hands. Everything you've held on to has
prepared you for this. Look at your calluses.

Harvey studies her hands as Iris runs her fingers over them.

IRIS

Think about the walls you'll paint.

*Iris lifts Harvey's hand out, extending it with Harvey's palm
out towards the house. Harvey drops the car.*

*Harvey looks at Iris and lifts her other palm out, closing her
eyes. Iris does the same.*

HARVEY

Maybe, I'll get a horse.

IRIS

(suddenly bright) Oooh! What color? What color?

HARVEY

Green, obviously.

IRIS

It'll match your apartment!

HARVEY

Who says I have to have an apartment? Maybe I'll really get a castle.

IRIS

Even I know you're too broke for that.

HARVEY

Well—

Harvey puts her hands down, keeping her eyes closed.

HARVEY

I can still have my bookshelf. At least seven feet tall.

Harvey rushes through the cabin as if she's drawing out what the space looks like with her eyes closed. Iris laughs and eyes closed, jumps on top of one of the chairs.

IRIS

Here's where you'll put the dining table.

HARVEY

Don't you think that's a little close to the wall?

IRIS

How many guests are you planning on having?

HARVEY

Hey, I did maybe make a friend today. She may or may not be a kid who also has an imaginary friend—

IRIS

Off to a great start. But what about the water slide?

Harvey runs across to the other side of the train car, eyes still closed.

HARVEY

Here, obviously! Right next to—

IRIS

The orchid garden!

HARVEY

I'll start with four.

Iris jumps down, eyes still closed.

IRIS

Only four?

HARVEY

What?

IRIS

That doesn't seem like enough.

HARVEY

You think I can take care of more without you?

IRIS

You did get that one to bloom in Orchid World.

HARVEY

Wait— We didn't imagine that?

IRIS

(beat) No. You took good care of it.

HARVEY

I— I didn't know that was real.

IRIS

Harvey, you love things enough to breathe life into them.

Harvey's eyes shoot open to the train cabin. She recognizes how empty it is, but seems like she's finally full of hope. She walks over and picks up Mikey's car, putting it in her pocket. Iris does not open her eyes.

IRIS

And here is the perfect spot for that green wall or maybe even a mural! A custom, Harvey original. *(beat) (grinning)* What do you think about that?

Harvey stares at Iris before walking over behind her and placing her hands on top of her shoulders. Harvey rests her head down beside Iris' closed eyes.

HARVEY

I think its perfect.

IRIS

This place looks brilliant! Don't you think?

Harvey looks around with open eyes, knowing Iris has imagined something brilliant. Knowing they have.

HARVEY

It does.

Iris, eyes still closed, tilts her head up in realization.

IRIS

You know, I never got to ask my question.

HARVEY

You better make it good.

Iris smiles softly, the two of them still standing center stage.

IRIS

I feel like mine's kinda silly.

HARVEY

There are no silly questions.

IRIS

Alright... *(beat)* Is the Orchid World Building still standing?

HARVEY

(beat) Last I remember it was.

IRIS

(grinning, finally opening her eyes) Good. I hope it stays.

HARVEY

(beat) Maybe it will.

There's a flicker of red light just before a cut to black.

Scene 6

Setting: *The main train cabin, morning*

At Rise: *The morning light breaks through the
train windows. All the passengers are asleep
in the chairs. Donna stirs first, sitting up
straight.*

DONNA

Like I couldn't be more uncomfortable.

*Mikey stirs in her seat and May sits up. Sammi is nowhere
to be seen.*

MAY

You sleep okay?

MIKEY

(groggy) Sammi kept kicking me in the back.

MAY

(stroking her hair) I'm sure she didn't mean to.

MIKEY

(to an invisible Sammi) Stop it!

*May takes Mikey's hands and she looks up at her, growing
still.*

MAY

You don't have to be her friend forever.

MIKEY

But Sammi's my best friend.

MAY

And you will make so many new friends.

MIKEY

No one's better than Sammi.

MAY

I know Mikey... *(gentle)* I know.

Enter Jack.

JACK

Good morning folks, we should be rolling into New York Grand Central in about fifteen minutes.

DONNA

Hallelujah.

Lewis nudges Harvey awake.

LEWIS

You're nearly to New York.

Harvey sits up straight.

JACK

Please gather your belongings.

Jack exits, walking through to the next cabin.

LEWIS

You made it.

Harvey turns and begins looking out the window at the rolling scenery. Her face lights up.

DONNA

Wait till you smell it. *(pulling out her phone)* Can't wait to get out of here.

LEWIS

It hasn't been that bad.

DONNA

Someone tried to literally kill themselves. And— people have been verbally accosting me. I didn't get any sleep. And I'm starving. *(to Harvey, condescending)* What time's your family meeting you?

HARVEY

(beat) I'm here solo. I think I'm moving here.

DONNA

Good luck with that.

HARVEY

Thank you.

DONNA

You know you could lose more than a book here. You're your only ally, that's it. It's just—

HARVEY

Real. *(beat)* I know.

Harvey looks down at her hands, tracing the callous on her palm.

Donna turns back and starts packing her bag up. Lewis turns to Harvey.

LEWIS

Any luck finding your book?

Harvey shakes her head.

HARVEY

(beat) I can get another copy.

Jack enters the cabin.

JACK

Alright folks, please line up by the front door. Thank you for traveling with us, we hope to see you again.

DONNA

You will not.

JACK

I've heard.

Jack nods to Harvey and exits.

HARVEY

Are you excited to meet your daughter's girlfriend?

LEWIS

I'm actually a little nervous... Sounds like this girl might be the one.

HARVEY

You're gonna do great.

Donna pulls down her suitcase. On the front of it, there is an embroidered orchid flower.

HARVEY

Is that an orchid?

DONNA

(cold) Yes, it is.

HARVEY

(nodding) They're my favorite flower.

DONNA

(unimpressed) You and everybody else these days.

HARVEY

A friend and I used to take care of some.

DONNA

I haven't met anyone that can take care of them like I do. Or... Did.

Donna looks over the bag.

DONNA

(beat) I owned a place that only sold orchids. It had been a dream of mine, but... It closed a long time ago.

HARVEY

(shocked) Was it called... Orchid World? Big purple castle-type building?

Donna's eyes narrow.

HARVEY

I— that building was... Really special to me.

DONNA

My ex-husband says it's an eye-sore.

HARVEY

I didn't think so.

DONNA

Well... *(beat)* Not a lot of money in fantasy businesses.

HARVEY

I'd love to see what it would look like with some life inside again.

DONNA

(beat) Maybe it was ahead of it's time.

HARVEY

You never know.

The train horn blares, gradually rolling to a stop.

JACK

Arriving at Grand Central Station!

The passengers begin shuffling towards the front of the train. Mikey jumps up and runs into the aisle. She picks up Harvey's book from the floor.

MIKEY

Miss!

Harvey turns and sees the book in her hands, her eyes widening.

LEWIS
(nudging Harvey) What did I say?

Harvey walks over to Mikey and takes the book from her, looking it over in her hands.

MIKEY
Maybe you did drop it.

Harvey studies the book and reads the note inside the front cover before closing it. Harvey turns to May, holding out the book to her.

HARVEY
Mikey can have this. I've read it more times than I can count. *(she holds up Mikey's car)* Consider it a trade.

MAY
Are you sure?

HARVEY
It might help her with Sammi someday.

May stares at Harvey.

MAY
You think?

HARVEY
I do.

May looks the book over. Mikey jumps up and down holding her hands out to an invisible Sammi.

MIKEY

The funny book! The funny book! See Sammi, I told you she was nice.

MAY

(beat) Thank you.

Harvey grins and then kneels down so she's on eye-level with Mikey.

HARVEY

I hope you and Sammi have the best time at your dad's house, okay?

MIKEY

Sammi says we're going to race cars the whole time.

HARVEY

I hope you do.

MAY

Come on Mikey... Thanks again.

May and Mikey exit the train. Donna, Lewis, and Harvey shuffle to the front of the line.

HARVEY

Maybe you can get a flight next time.

DONNA

Oh, I'm never boarding a God-forsaken train ever again. *(beat)* Thanks for— Thanks. Been a long time since I daydreamed about that place.

Donna's phone begins to ring.

DONNA

(into her phone) Casey... Casey I'm at the station. You'd better be close—

Donna hobbles off the train. Lewis hands Harvey a piece of paper.

LEWIS

Now, call me if you need anything. I won't have you sleeping on the street.

HARVEY

(laughs) Yes sir.

LEWIS

You got a strong head on your shoulders, good on your for using it.

HARVEY

I think I'm ready.

LEWIS

(stepping off the train) Does anybody really know when they're ready? We all just—

HARVEY

—jump.

Lewis nods, exits, leaving Harvey alone on the train.

VOICE
Last call for Grand Central Station, this is the last call for
Grand Central Station!

*Harvey looks around and the lights above her flicker red,
just for a moment.*

She grins, and steps off the train.

END OF PLAY.

Vanessa Frances is an Orlando-based playwright and author specializing in speculative, reality-focused fiction that delves into the complexities of human experience amidst societal and environmental upheavals. She holds a BA in Digital Journalism and Media from Pennsylvania State University and certifications in Creative Writing from the University of Central Florida and Sustainable Business from Cornell University. *The Magic Castle Still Stands* won Patron's Pick at Orlando Fringe 2024. Her writing has been featured in Forbes, Canary Media, and Storyteller Literary Magazine. She is the author of *Through Neighboring Windows* and *Orange Island*.